THESE A

I TOLD YOU

KERRY HAMMERTON

THESE ARE THE

I TOLD YOU

KERRY HAMMERTON

Copyright © Kerry Hammerton 2010

First published in October 2010 by Modjaji Books

P O Box 385, Athlone, 7760, Cape Town, South Africa

http://modjaji.book.co.za

modjaji.books@gmail.com

ISBN 978-1-920397-22-7

Book and cover design by Jacqui Stecher

Printed and Bound by Mega Digital, Cape Town

Set in Joanna

for my mother who taught me
to love books
and for worm – uh oh!

contents

When all the mysteries are revealed

We are a slow unfolding,
a soft pencil nudging
the crumpled folds of a manuscript,
a sable brush sweeping sand
from Dead Sea scrolls,
a Timbuktu book.

I am afraid that
when all the mysteries are revealed:
the feel of a first kiss,
the location of that tattoo
surgery scars, toothpaste brands,
plain cotton underwear;

it could all be over.

There is only this

Bed covers thrown back to reveal
all the nooks and spaces of our bodies.
Ben upstairs knocking on the floor,
inviting us for a late afternoon drink.

You holding my back with the span
of your hands, dark eyes smiling,
my lips tugging up in response.
Deep belly laughs rocking us closer.

Later we'll lie joined by skin, there will be
less of us and more of you and more
of me. Yet no moving, no going,
no separation and yet, all of these things.

You'll get up to make us tea, run me
a bath, call your mother. Even later
I'll be able to see your freckles
clearly from across the table.

Things
I've
left
behind
in
hotel
rooms

rumpled sheets

crushed pillows

beach sand in the bath

drawn curtains

an overturned wine glass

the steady drip drip drip from an unclosed tap

a blank TV screen

wet towels on the floor

a sticky puddle of champagne

unanswered telephone calls

an abandoned room service tray

water footprints on the carpet

lathered soap

a silent alarm clock

time exhausted with you

You left me a note once

Found Poem

It said:

'you got so close to me,
so quickly,
with such ease,
how did I ever allow it?
All the craziness,
the easy laughter,
the uncomplicated
conversation,
the loving,
the learning,
all we have
comes from you,
your magic
and my response
to you.
I don't want to be inside
emptiness again.
Thank you for showing me
the me
that I thought
was missing.

I love you'

The sickness of us

It is time that we stood up,
up and out of this indolent bed
where we have consumed each other.
No toe, no thought, no breast,
no piece of skin, no memory,
no rib untouched
as if life has no breath apart.
It 's time we stood up.

The leaves are wearing
their autumn colours, the play
we planned to see in the summer
is holding its closing show.
We've missed the cricket season,
the blockbuster movie of the year,
books lie unread, friends unseen,
did we visit our families at Christmas?

The windows look dusty,
the front door stuck
from dis-use, the dog's dead
from neglect,
the electricity and water
have been cut off,
they've disconnected our phone.

Let us bottle up this room,
the sweat and sex stained sheets,
coffee cups littering the floor,
discarded dressing gowns,
the bed where we have
created storms, marooned.

It's time we got up,
it's time we got over this sickness.

A modern love poem

You are a red jacket in the winter cold,
a beach umbrella in the sun,
a black cocktail dress on an evening out,
a frozen margarita , a chilled glass
of white wine, worn-in slippers,
a warm dressing gown.

You are a fresh coat of paint on the wall,
a candle in a blackout,
comfortable takkies on a morning run,
a hot water bottle, an extra blanket,
a cup of roasted coffee, rooibos tea,
a slice of chocolate cake.

You are the windscreen wipers in the rain,
the flowers blooming in the spring,
green traffic lights when I am running late,
a glitter gel pen, jeans that fit,
mulled red wine, hot chocolate
a book of poems.

You are an unexpected cheque in the post,
a rainbow on a cloudy day,
the first sighting of whales for the year,
a new notebook, port and cigars,
the crunch of popcorn, peach gardenias,
a crackling fire.

You are the smile on a baby's face,
a landrover on a bush drive,
the mist and rain on a snuggle-in day,
the latest novel, a comedy film,
purple dancing shoes, a sharp knife,
a flight of penguins.

Familiarity

After a day spent
tip-tattooing your fingers
across a keyboard
that doesn't know
the order of the alphabet,
you lie beside me.
Arms and legs rigid,
your back has become
your new face.

Let me breathe on you,
let the whispers from
my mouth flex you, yield you.

If I trace my fingers along
the unseen line that runs
down from your nipple, let

them ski along the soft contours of
your ribs, stroke the almost pubic
hair on your belly, drift downwards
to almost touching, not quite

and all the while my mouth
is dancing the tango with yours,

you will rise up to welcome me.

Marriage bed

Laid out cold on a slab,
pubic hair curling
in the harsh overhead light,
hips vulnerable,
my breasts droop to the side.

You poke an indifferent
finger into my exposed
ribs,
speak in funny voices
and then fart, belch,
as if I wasn't in the room.

If you held my hand,
stroked your fingers lightly up
my wrist, kissed
my lips with your hot mouth,
I would open for you.

Why are you so irritable?

You forgot to pick up the socks you discarded
while watching TV last night. Drank the last bit of
milk just before bed and put the empty bottle back.

I'm not really. Just tired. I've had
a long day. You know how it is.

It took me two hours to clean up the mess
you made in the kitchen after you cooked
a cholesterol stimulating supper last night.
I'm still ten kilos overweight and on a diet.

Am I really? Gosh, I didn't notice.
It must be this hot and windy weather.

You got drunk and silly on Friday night.
Annoyed my boss. I've already been waiting
three weeks for my promotion letter.

I've got a headache. I don't mean to be.
I think I'll go lie down until the feeling passes.

You went down to the pub on Saturday
to watch a match, didn't come home.
Forgot we were going out to see your friends..

Someone tried to cut me off in traffic.
Missed me by inches. Scared me.

You never say thank you.

I must be getting my period

All the things I don't know how to do

Haggle at the fish market,
lean into a dying sea
smell to claim a few pennies.
Rollerblade. Run with the bulls.
Swim with the current. Stay cool
in the summer. Hold my breath.
Warm this silence between us.

You photograph me

fatten my face,
draw middle-aged lines
on my brow,

deepen the contours that
furrow down from my nose,
double my chin.

Only in my eyes
do I see
me.

I said something profound

But you'd already turned to watch
ducks paddling against the tide,
almost standing still in the wash
of water flowing away from them.

Saying goodbye

You line them up
neatly in a row
across the table:
Mrs Ball's Chutney
Original Recipe,
All Gold Tomato
Sauce, organic
sea salt, whole
black pepper, HP
sauce and your
favourite Tabasco:

you like one drop
in the middle of
each egg. Sunny
side up. The bottles
clink nervously.
You finally lift
your head.

Later your empty
chair creates
a space
for the hiss
of the coffee
steamer and
teaspoons to
clang against
cups and saucers.

My hands call
for the bill.
The door
softly sucks
itself closed
behind me.

Hangover Cure

I still use your hangover cure:

a tall glass of water
before bed and then
in the morning:

first something salty,
scrambled eggs and toast,
crispy bacon; second
something sweet.

And then coffee.

Throughout the day
small regular meals.

Alternating salt
and sweet. Salt
and sweet. Salt
and sweet.

Shoes

His shoes lie crumpled
and abandoned at the foot
of the bed. Every pair he owns.

I stumble over them, once
a day, twice a day, three
times a day, maybe even more.

I curse him then.
Pretend he still lives here,
with his shoes.

Suffused

I fold the things I want to take:

Sunday morning breakfasts
dissecting the newspaper, holding
hands as we crossed the road,
mountain walks, your raised
eyebrow when you were perplexed
or angry, scuba diving in Zanzibar,
playing old-fashioned pinball
at one o'clock in the morning,
the mole behind your knee,
you in my pink dressing gown
because yours was in the wash,
your mouth on my breast,
the smell of your neck,
the time you disrupted my
bridge evening because you
couldn't wait to see me,
the way you always yelled:
'Honey, I'm home',
the eighty roses
you gave me once,
the feel of your arm
on my shoulder.

Drifting between the us
of then and the us of now,
I become suffused
with the certainty of who I am.

Come visit, have coffee

What I mean is:

come visit, hold my hand;
take an hour just to stroke
the skin around my belly
button; another to trace
the path up to my sternum;
another hour to tickle
the hollows in my back.

And then if you want,
and I'm not too tired,
lie next to me, fit your
knees in their place
behind mine and
let me feel the comfort
of your lap.

Diary of a relationship

It happened on a Monday: heels
head tumble over: my grey eyes
blue, slow your smile; streaked
hair sun my; your lashes long.

On Tuesday I knew the regiment
your granddad served in during
the war, the name of your childhood
pet, a diamond sparkle on my finger.

On Wednesday it was confetti,
a white dress, you intoxicated from
your bachelor party, tolling church bells.

On Thursday a promise
of a child that slipped away,
never to be conceived of again.

On Friday we travelled overseas,
indulged at the spa, reached
a truceful companionship,
tried to harmonise diaries.

Saturday: tears,
voices raised,
mysterious
disappearances.

On Sunday I woke up,
forty years old, single
again, you becoming
a dad for the first time.

Wedding day blues

I'm caught in traffic
this morning: no electricity,
no breakfast tea.

The cars in front at ease in the shade.

Battered by the air conditioner
the petrol gauge drops
millimeter by millimeter.

I have to pat and tousle
my drying hair in place.

The stone spire rises above
the trees – there just ahead,
can you see it?

We crawl a few more paces.

The digital figures on the dashboard flash
again and again; I'm going to be late.

A break and we jump two car lengths,
slam to a halt, indicators flare,
trying to get out of the slow lane.

A red car turns off the road
but I'm stuck.   Stopping
and starting with the flow.

We move suddenly, I'm beside the church,
she's barbie doll pretty, laughing
at her white veil in the wind.

And then I am past, unbelievably, inexplicably, free.

Survival

the sea beckons me into
its soft death,

only the thought of that
something unresolved
between us,

keeps my feet in my shoes.

Long Street : Cape Town

Night leaches out heat
gathered in my bones,
shuts down the day with
a clash of roller-shutter doors.
Raindrops glisten on cars
as they swish and hoot
their way home.
The barman is playing Billy Joel.

Smoke from a wet-wooded fire
drifts closer, someone lights
a joint and young lovers kiss
as the moon claims its place
in the night. Music spins into
a throb. Mini-skirted girls charm
the barman. I smile. He smiles.
They always pay full price.

Lurid signs on the street grapple
for attention. Leather jacketed
men, wolves in sheep skin,
tuck women around them. Here
I remember you, beer bottle
raised, wide smile, freckles,
your fingers linked through mine.

The barman calls final round.

Love

No clichéd roses on Valentine's day.
No chocolate hearts. No frothed
moustaches over a cup of cappuccino.
No irritation. No summer picnics
in bed. No noisy breakfast TV just
to catch the weather. No telephone
calls to tell a joke. No deep bellied laughs.
No personal smiles. No weekends away.
No beery friends. No rugby braais.
No teenage fumblings on the couch.
No passionate kisses. No hello.
No goodbye. No slow sex. No fighting
for the duvet in winter. No fighting.
No crazy dancing at one a.m. on drunken
city streets. No marriage proposal.
No mother-in-law. No house.
No Labrador. No fast sex. No sex.
No driving too fast. No thinking
when he leaves the house,
jacketed and tie'd up:
glad he's coming home.

Song

(in response to Christina Rossetti)

When I am dead, my dearest,
roll out the mourning carpet,
muffle black horses' hooves,
draw my coffin in a gilded carriage
through every town and village.

Buy all the roses in all the colours
from every florist. Festoon my last path
with the scent of crushed petals.

Hire a gospel choir, a praise singer,
professional mourners to rent
their clothes and tear out their hair.

Throw yourself into the maw
of my grave as the coffin is lowered,
keen your wretchedness to the sky.

Let mottled circles grow under your eyes,
don't wash or comb your hair for weeks.

I want you to stroll in the rain, wear
black, kiss my cold, cold lips everyday.

Medical Emergency

They called an ambulance.
Rushed me to the trauma unit,
examined me in haste,
summoned all the experts, the specialists,
organised a video conference
with the Swiss doctors,
the American doctors,
but they couldn't diagnose,
- shrugging shoulders,
showing empty palms,
ordering tests.

After blood had been taken,
toxicology screens, hair analysis,
intestinal scopes, x-rays, ECGs,
the MRI scan found it: a tiny
fold in the tissue of my brain.
An 'engram' they called it,
shaking hands, slapping backs,
congratulating each other,
nodding wisely. Go home
they said, we will never
be able to cure you.

I wanted brain surgery,
heart surgery. Rotating saws,
the smell of charred bone,
fine cauterising instruments,
scalpels, a swell of blood, rock
music playing in the background.
Go home they said. Go home.
There is no pill, no surgery,
no diet, no syrup, no injection,
no doctor, no surgeon, no midwife
no healer, no sangoma able
to expunge the memory of him.

Thank you Rochelle for encouraging
me to buy super-control lycra paneled
hold-it-all-in whale-boned silhouette
enhancing tummy tucking guaranteed
to leave no panty-line support knickers

I wear them every day.

One minute lover

A blue arm encircles me.
I feel the kiss of his shirt against my hand,
thigh pressed against mine.
I strain forward,
I long to lean back,
feel his chest,
be absorbed
by his heat,
hear gasps,
hair entangled,
his breath
warm on my neck.

The train lurches and stops.
He is gone.

Jellyfish lover

He bites, he stings,
wraps his tentacles

around your heart.
Raises red welts

on your skin.
You always dive back

into the tumble surf,
wanting more.

You taught me

You taught me to be naked.
Wake up and tumble out of bed,
breasts swaying, make coffee,

serve you a topless breakfast.
After this shameless display
there would be a return

to warm sheets, a delight
in the hairy rub of your leg.
You taught me to make

pasta with the barest hint
of tarragon and exotic fungi.
And a three cheese sauce.

You taught me to listen to
Cuban Jazz. You taught me
about French restaurants,

the different flavours in red wine.
You taught me that a married
man never leaves his wife.

Beach sex

It's a chill night. Sea breeze smells
and grasses. Sand slides under our feet.
We find a space behind a dune,
hands catch and fumble.

We're startled by the sound
of deep African hymns.
You hush me in my fear.

A sand crab scuttles away
pincers menacing in the dark.

The roar of the waves drowns
out the sounds that say
I'm desperate to please you.

I catch a glimpse of something
pale and white. I've escaped
from my body, moving like a ghost
across the landscape.

From a different coast you came to me

I brushed sand from your back
everyday, my hand entangled in
long green fronds clinging to your
shoulders, your skin like volcanic
lava cooled in a salt blue sea,

The strength of your desire rushed
over me, giddy with possibilities.
When my desire opened up, you
sang lullabies to slow me down.

My skin was scented with your skin –
old rum and sharp fresh lime.

You shadowed the landscape
of my world, took things,
spliced them with your body
growing oddly angled and round.

Sand didn't stick on your grey suit
but you always got up to watch
the shadows behind your eyes.

When I hold my hands over my ears
now I hear the sea.

I'd take more care

You drove all that way. Eleven thousand
kilometres. Your car clicking and bending
in the heat. The house overrun with a

rubber smell of flip-flops, wet sand
encrusted towels, shoes discarded
like old bones, arms, legs, the taste of

suntan lotion on our watermelon skin.
Sand in the roots of my hair. Your hand
easily held my hands, spanned my back,

rough against my skin, my nose buried
in the salted hair of your armpit. I
remember the cinnamon of your

aftershave, the slippery sea taste of
your tongue, your indrawn breath like
silk across my skin. If I knew you now

Aubade

You've unbroken the egg,
unfiltered the coffee,
unbuttered the toast.

Your fridge shut
against the light.

Less a merging,
(entwined limbs
and whispers of breath)

more a positioning
(mashed limbs
and false sighs).

Your snore bristled
the hairs in my ears.

You pushed me out of bed.
No more honey.
No more baby.

No more.

You've tumbled me up.

Luck

It is such amazing luck you said,
bumping into you again.
And again.
And again.
And again.

I think that you keep turning up
like a bad penny.

Undergarments

Bra, panties, you're in my fantasy.
Garters, stockings, it's really quite shocking.
Negligee, teddy, I'm quite ready.
Silk, satin, let's make it happen.
Whips? Mask? Maybe we're going too fast.

Once I knew

A porky- pie, a flirst,
a man whose appetite was bigger that his thirst.

A smargy-smark, a flowel,
a man who couldn't pick up a towel.

A dringy-drogue, a cheddle,
a man who really liked to meddle.

Once I knew

a spreaky-spreck, a growlth,
a man who couldn't shut his mouth.

A reepy-rost, a jost,
a man who was always lost.

A marfy-makker, a mhale
a man who confessed and went to jail.

Once I knew

a peedle-pudum, a shile,
a man who couldn't smile.

A hirgy-hattle, a brister
a man who was all a pister,

a fleety-fluster, a basfitter,

a lespy-lerper, a verter,

a crutter, a creter,

a werter.

But worst of all, once I knew

a mishy-mashy, welljuten,

a zandripertosster.

How Many Times Must I say Goodbye?

Give you the old heave-ho?
Say toodle – loo?
Arrivederci? Adieu?
Au revoir?
Maybe if I try it in Spanish?
Adios. German?
Auf Wiedersehen.
Turkish? I think not.
It's over. Goodbye.

If

If my credit card hadn't just expired, and you
weren't just getting a divorce. If I had

been able to find the bank and you didn't
live in the area. If I hadn't turned into that

car-park, and you hadn't just been to the doctor.
If I hadn't walked across the tarmac, and you

hadn't recognized the back of my head.
If I hadn't been in love with you, years ago,

and if that had changed in the intervening time.
If you hadn't asked and I had said no to coffee.

If we hadn't gone out on Friday night

Lust

The tide of you pulls me in
like a full moon. I am the horse
on your carousel, the desert
battering at your oasis.

Sugar baby

I am eating slabs
of chocolate torte,
sugared plums,
sticky figs,
dates,
licking gobs of honey
from my plate,

just to rouse
the taste of you.

Each time

I forget how your nostrils flare
just so, the cool porcelain
of your skin, the tiny tendrils
that curl on the damp
of your forehead at the end of the day.
The strength in your fingers, the arch
of your arm as it settles
on my shoulders, the huskiness
of your voice as you whisper
in my ear, the fullness of your lips as they
brush against my neck,
the way that you walk.
Each time I see you,
it's like the first time.

My body

'i like my body when it is with your body'

e.e. cummings

I like the way it yearns towards you,
the way it twists to absorb the flow of your thoughts,
and drinks in parts of you that you give away:

a careless squeeze of my shoulder;
a gentle touch of my wrist;
the brush of your arm against my back;
your fingers trailing across my belly.

Maybe its only purpose is to absorb
the words that you throw like darts
to pierce and poison my skin with love.

The sound of you

My body wants to sway to your rhythm,
flash a red flamenco dress with fingers
clicking across the floor, toss my head,
mesmerize you with my smouldering eyes.

Yet we dance a prosaic samba:
both of us looking the other way
our feet finding the rhythm, a step
forward, a step back, a polite step to the side.

My body wants to move to the sound
of you: dance a Mesemba or a Carioca;
feel a Conga, a Carnivale.

On realising
I'm in love with you

I wanted a man with a tall stride and
berry brown legs.
An adventurer.

A long-haired surfer with an earing
and a six-pack.
A self-made man.

A millionaire. A be-spectacled genius.
I am sure my ad said:
'must love dogs'.

And I got you.

How are babies made?

Your four year old voice asks from the backseat.
I am your aunt, and yes, your godmother but I have
had no training for this. So I stumble over silly words of
mommy's eggs and daddy's seeds and mommy's tummy.

But how does the baby get there?

The performance is easy: penis, vagina,
insertion, ejaculation, man, woman, orgasm.

But how do I tell you of the delight, of the taste
of someone else's skin, how you will caress each
part of him, how the curved husk of his ear
will astonish you, how your breath will quicken?

How do I tell you that the best part is when he holds
your hand, and murmurs your name, and kisses you
again and again. And again and again?

Our first time

I remember the hunger of your mouth
on my nipples the most.
You held me solid between your thighs,

unlocked a space connecting us,
biting lips on my neck,
velvet fingers brushing my back,

you pulled me you deep into me.
Woke me at three o'clock
hands stroking my breasts,

nipples standing once more
to your attention.
Later you walked me to my car,

feet picking across
sharp gravel, your naked chest chill
in the fresh morning air.

Identity

Sometimes I believe this is me
striding in my sharp black suit,
high heels, across the tarmac
to work, dodging cars as I
jaywalk my morning cardboard
coffee. Lodged in the centre of
my brain is a daily dirge
of meetings and a colour
coded to-do list.

And then late at night, cross
legged on the carpet, opposite
you drugged smoke drifting
between us words floating,
you pull me over,
and then in my bed
tangled sheets and sweat,
skin on skin,
that me is lost.

Halloween

She-devils in red dresses
leer over you.
Their ripe curves
nuzzling your face.
Tails and horns a-twitching.

They polish each word
you throw their way,
stretch their necks
and purr
at your school-boy jokes.

I sit quiet,
waiting to go home.

Tattoo

Because love can be so
unpredictable,

I would like to needle a tattoo
in the hollow of your throat:

a strawberry heart
to beat in tune
with the inflection of your pulse;

and in the web
between your forefinger
and your thumb:

a love bite
to remind you
of me.

Unlike you

I know how to return a call.
To be fair, maybe in this world
of modern technology you didn't
get my message: not the one
I left on your cell phone, not the
one I left on your land line.
not the email I sent.

Maybe I need to send you
detailed instructions:
Use your left hand to pick up
the phone, your right index finger
to press the numbered buttons in
the following sequence:
zero two one seven six two......

But: how will I get this message to you?

Mending me

My life unravels itself
centimeter by centimeter.
I want to wind it up.
Find the place where
you and I made sense.

In about six months

(But maybe it will really take
more than a year)

You will no longer have dominion,
the power to besiege and beguile me.
I will no longer be in love with you.

I am sure I will be over us, over you.

And the day after: when I go
shopping, take a trip to the laundry,
turn a corner, there you'll be.

My hands will want to run over your
jaw, feel the stubble on your chin.
My mouth will want to kiss your lips,
softly bite your neck. My eyes will close
(briefly) as I breathe you in, my body
will be aching to lean into yours.

On Losing You

I'm cast adrift in a storm
of my own making:
words, anger, conversations
fleeting through my mind.
Christ have mercy,
send me an angel of calm.

I don't want to reel back
to find your heart
that hooked me.
I've lost it, lost you.
Christ have mercy,
where the hell have you gone?

There is a lure of you in
my bed, my car, the streets,
the city, the fucking stars.
Christ have bloody mercy,
please just let the memories fall.

These are the Lies I told you

I will love you forever.
You are important to me.
We will always be friends.

On finally realising he is an Arsehole

I put down the phone.

Winter

Even on blue
sky days,
there is rain.

I catch streaked
glimpses
of you,

turn my head.
You disappear
into mist.

I am waiting
for snow.

Planting olive trees

When you plant an Olive Tree
don't sing to it,
don't sing songs of stars and moons
and distant galaxies, don't lean
into its leafy ears and whisper
honey words, don't even mouth
'I love you', don't recite poems
of open valleys and journeys,
don't talk.

When you plant an Olive Tree
plant it away from other trees
and then: don't visit it,
don't entwine your arms through
its branches, don't place your
face against its patterned bark
or reach out your tongue and taste,
don't rub your back against its trunk
don't stroke it.

When you plant an Olive Tree
don't water it or shower it
with drops of dew, don't sprinkle
it with the watering can of your
love, don't pray for rain,
don't snake a hosepipe
over sheer mountains or
climb treacherous rock
to bring relief.

When you plant an Olive Tree
find the stoniest ground, don't
prepare the planting with
fertilizer and soft soil, don't mulch,
let its roots feel the harsh bite
of the earth, let it scrape
against jagged rocks, don't dust
rose petals on fresh white linen
before you bed it down.
Let it lie in sharp gravel.

When you plant an Olive Tree
don't cover it,
let it bend in the wind,
let its leaves crackle in the sun,
don't build a boma of comfort,
don't try and protect it with
your manly intentions,
let it struggle to find its own shade
let it shrivel.

Then it will bear fruit
for you.

I am not
an Olive Tree.

Acknowledgements

My parents whose unending support has been continuous in my life and who helped me to believe in myself.

Tamar Yoseloff at the London Poetry School, her encouragement planted the seed of possibility.

My Fairy Godmother who taught me to dream big and to take action when answers presented themselves.

Finuala Dowling who provided a lot of the answers, a wonderful environment to write and explore poetry, endless laughter, lots of wine, good grammar and constant encouragement and support. I don't have enough words to tell you how much this means to me.

All the members of Pleached Poetry and their endless tolerance of all my 'bed' poems: Liz Trew, Michael Keeling, Angela Prew, Elaine Edwards and Lise Day.

Colleen Higgs. Thank you for providing this opportunity for me and for all Modjaji poets. You are a true inspiration.

Some of the poems in this collection were previously published in the following South African literary journals *Carapace*, *New Coin*, *New Contrast* and on-line in *Litnet* and *Incwadi*.